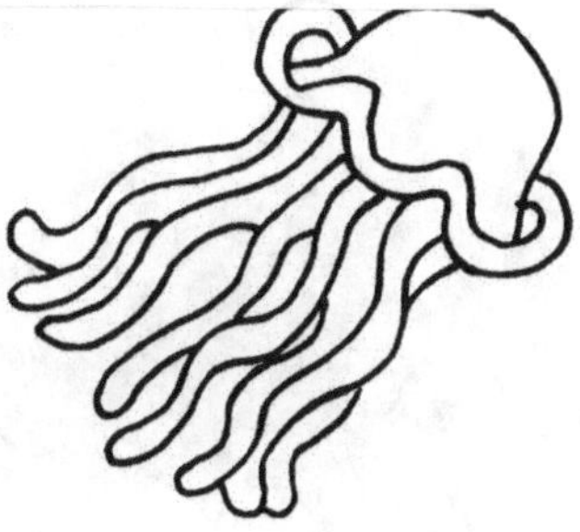

Coastal Creature Collection

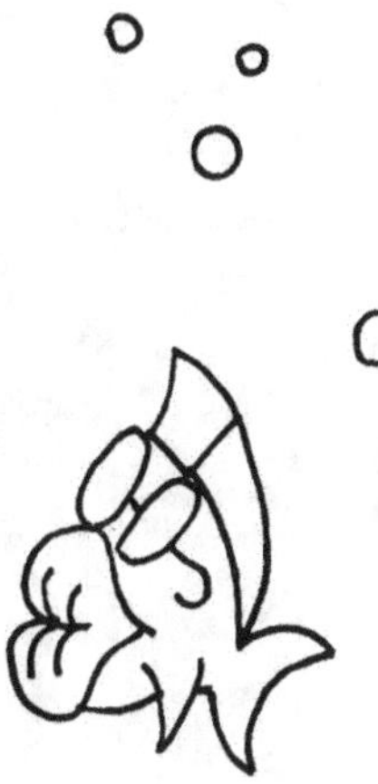

A fantastical coloring book

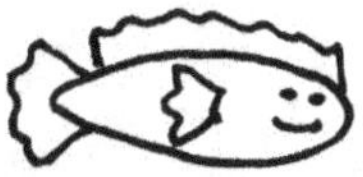

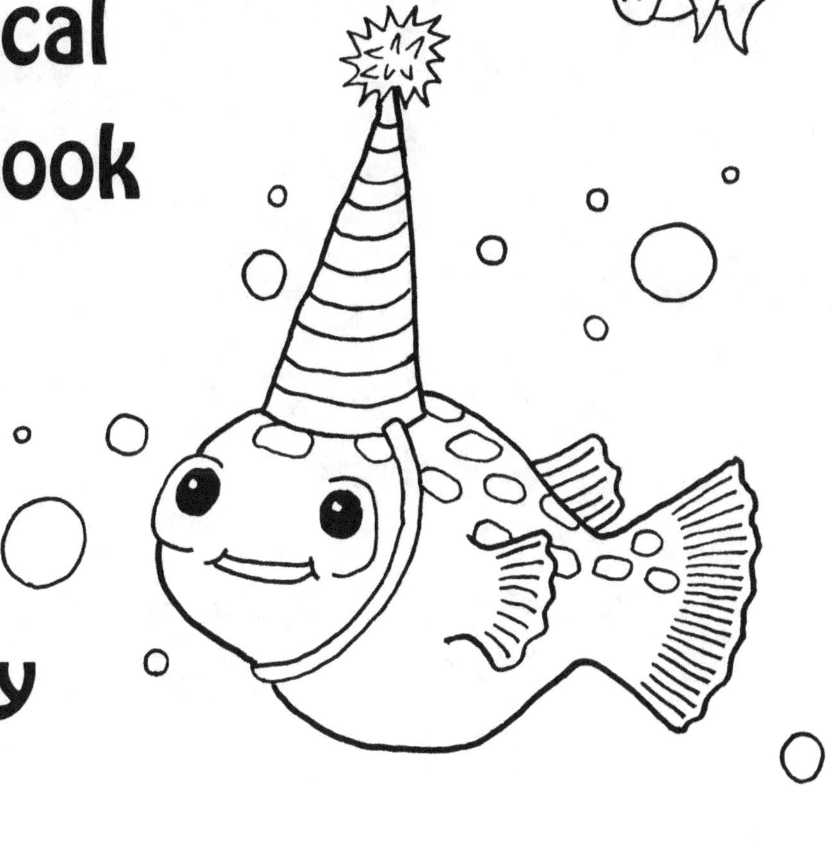

Created by
VA Roper

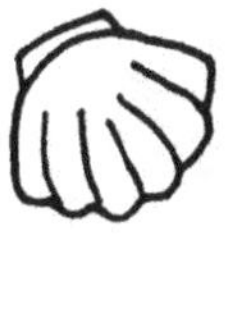

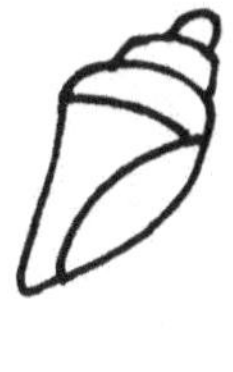

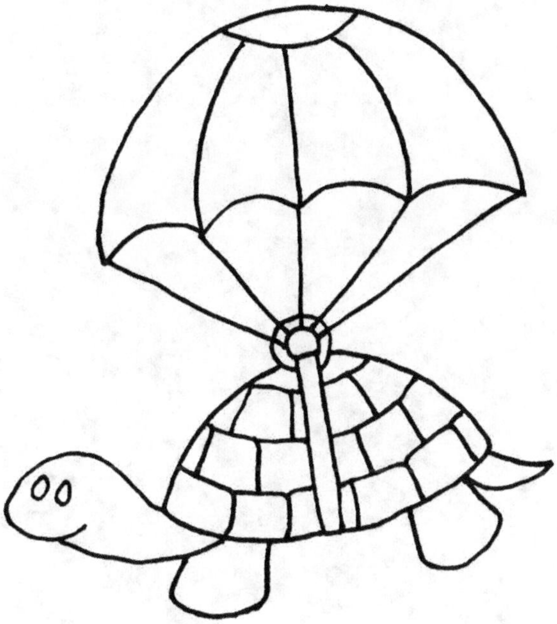

ISBN: 153997460X
ISBN-13: 978-1539974604

10 9 8 7 6 5 4 3 2 1
First Edition

See Virginia's other work at varoper.com.

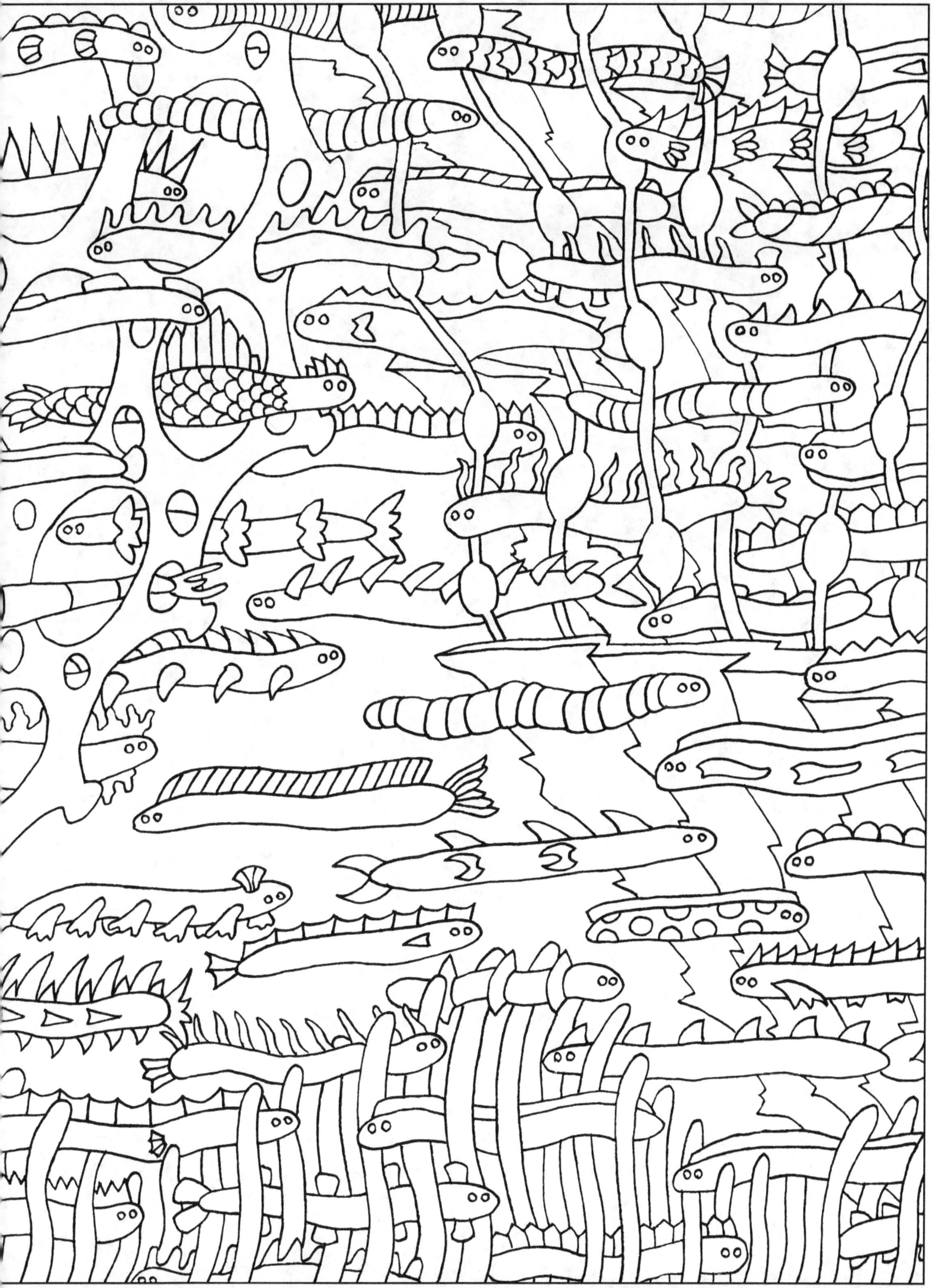

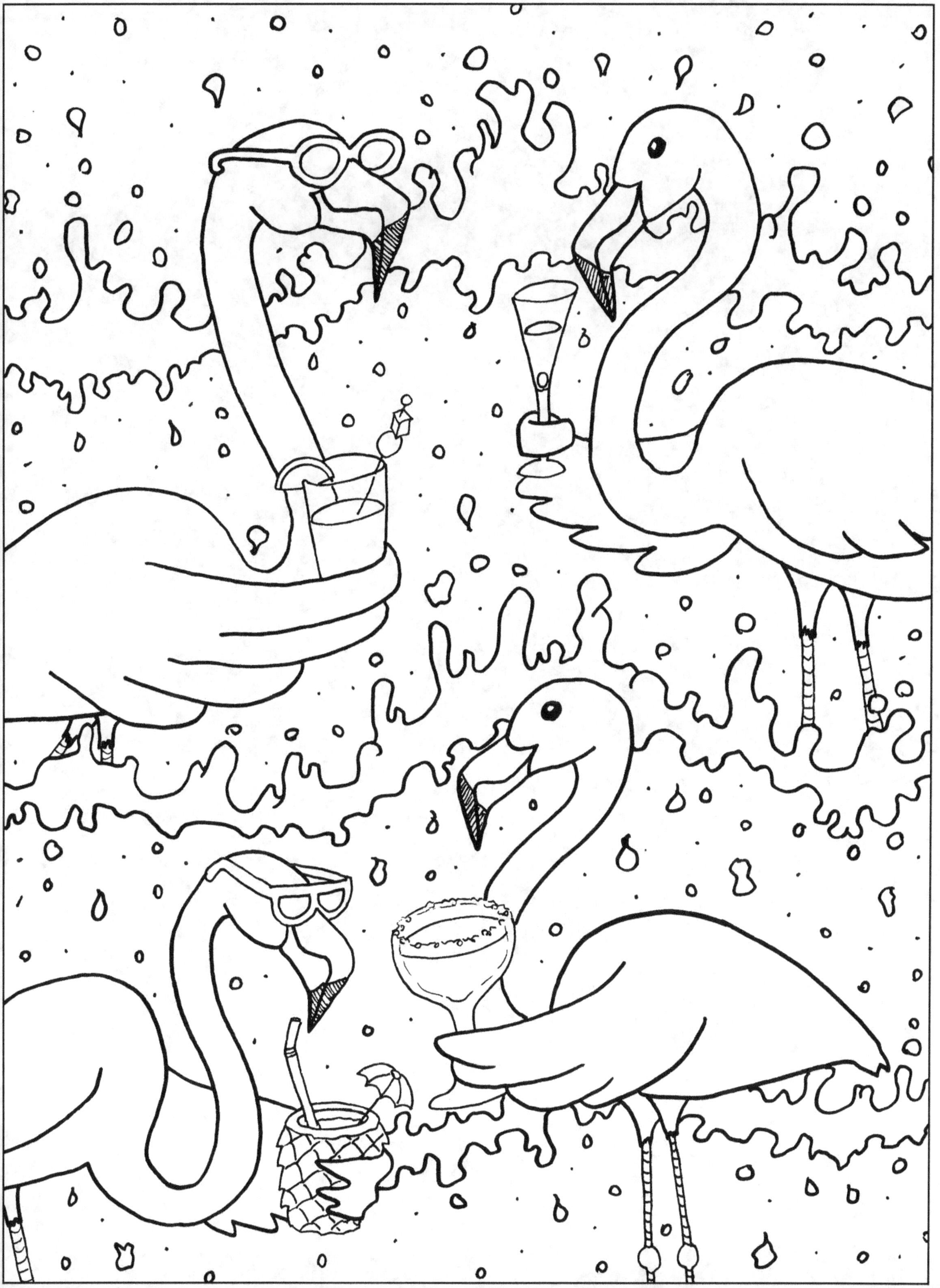

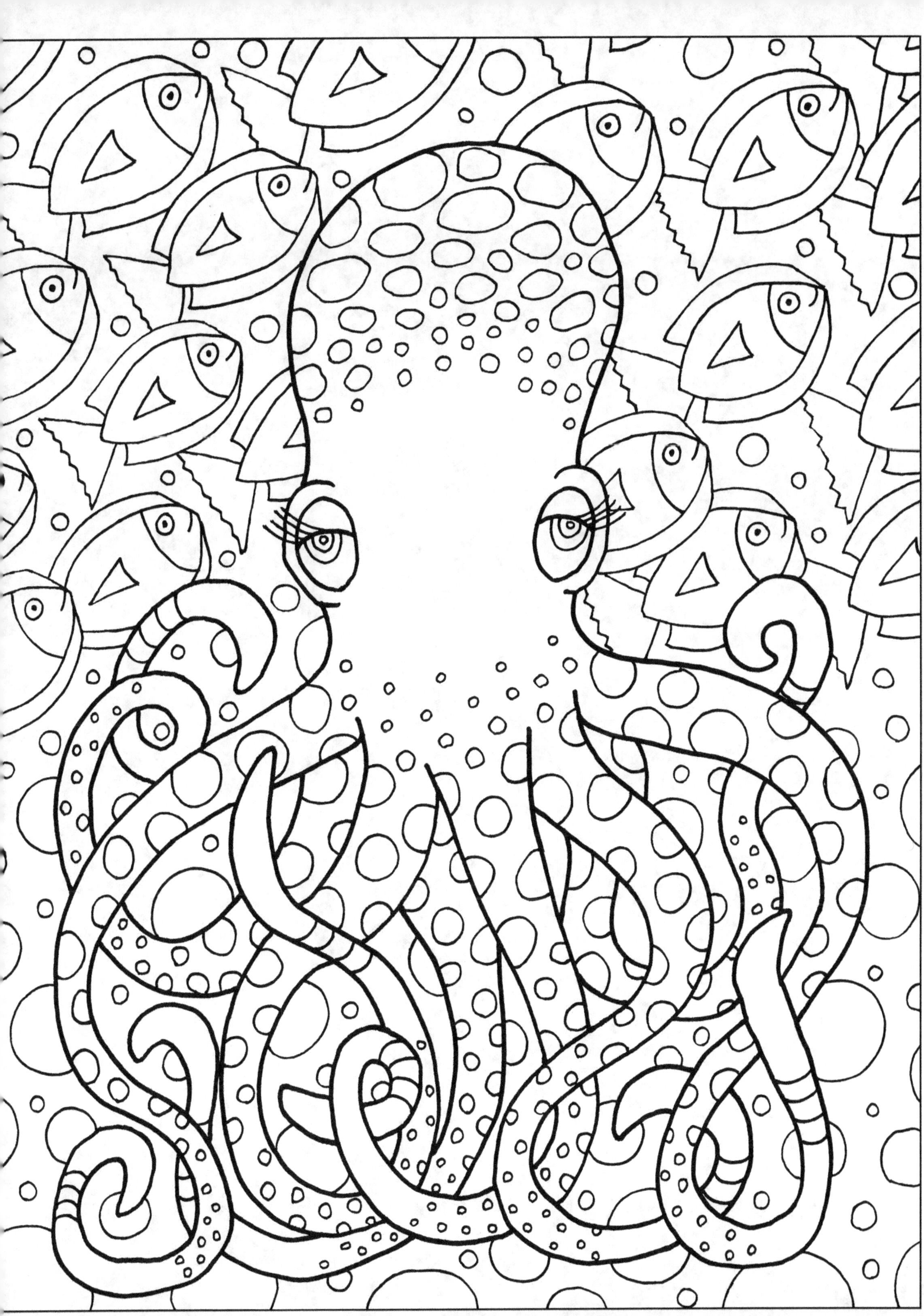

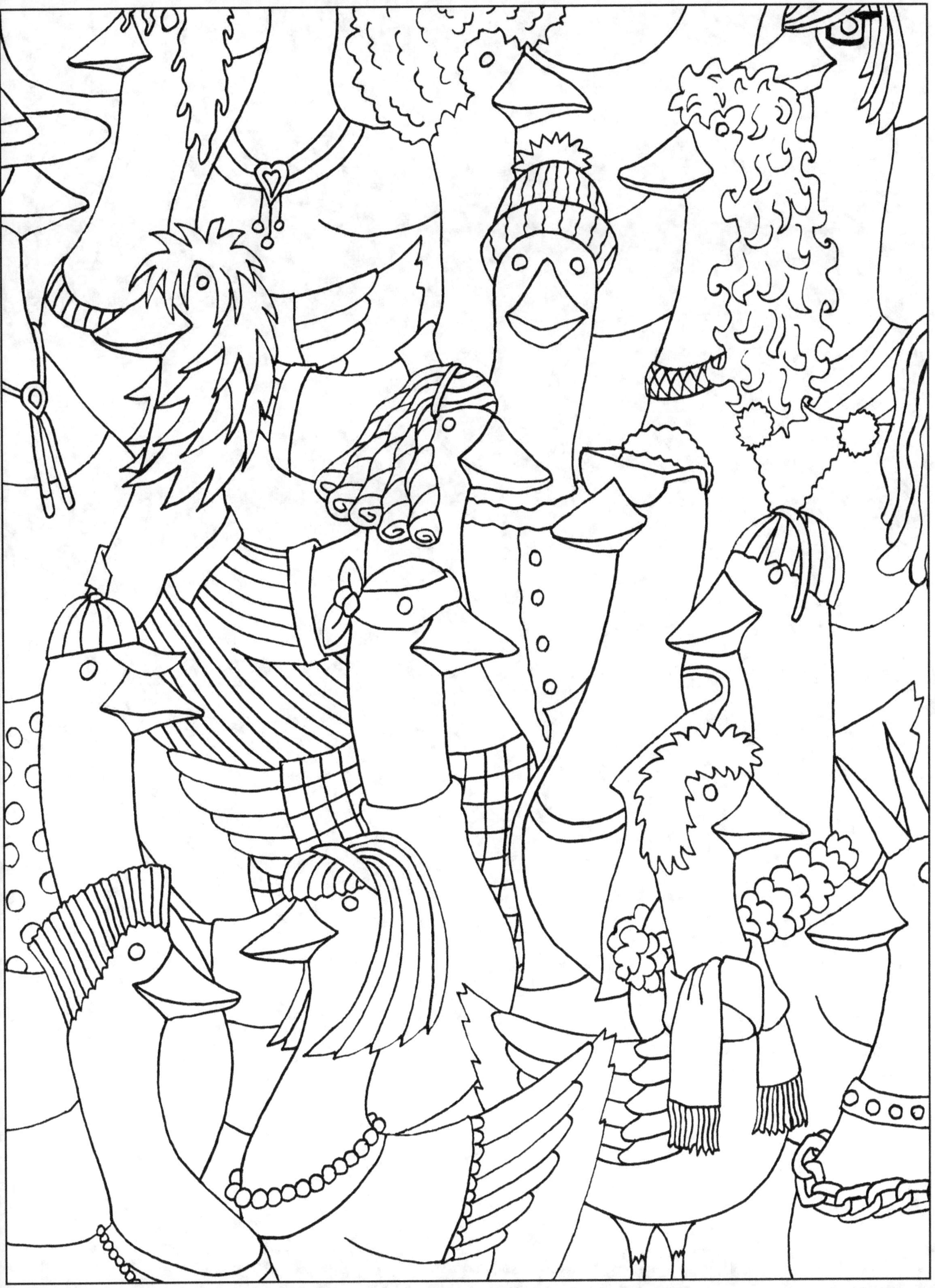

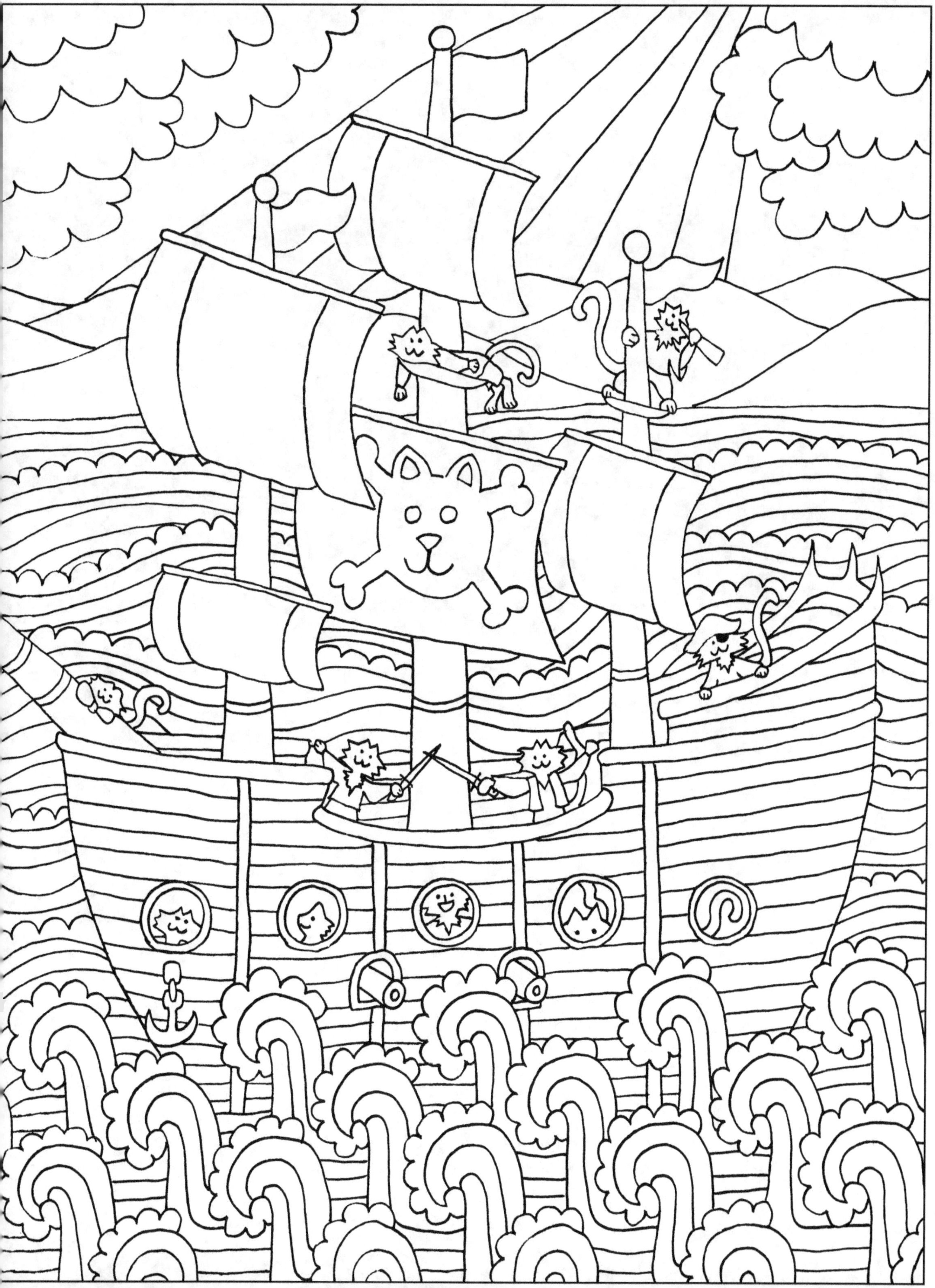

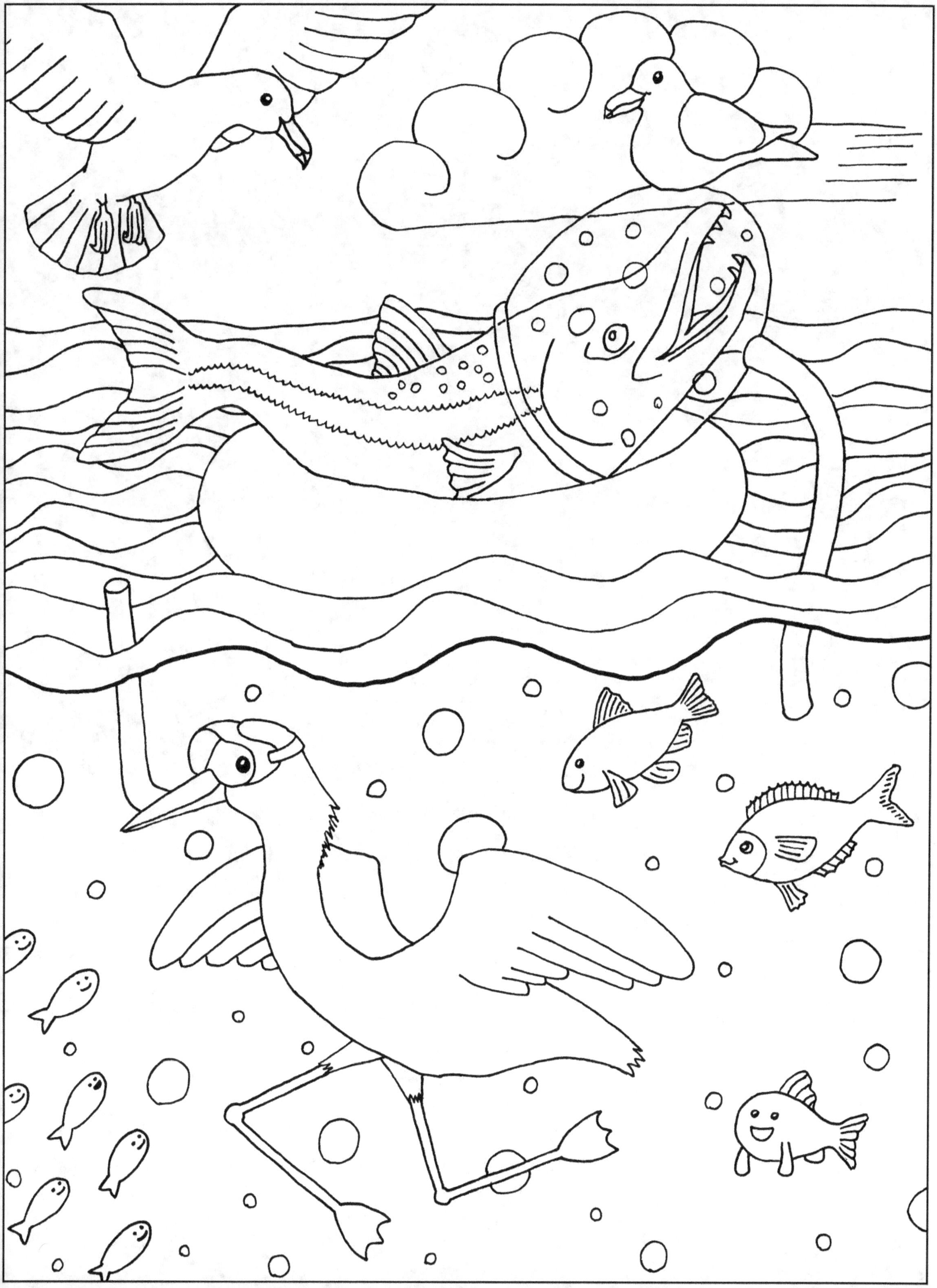

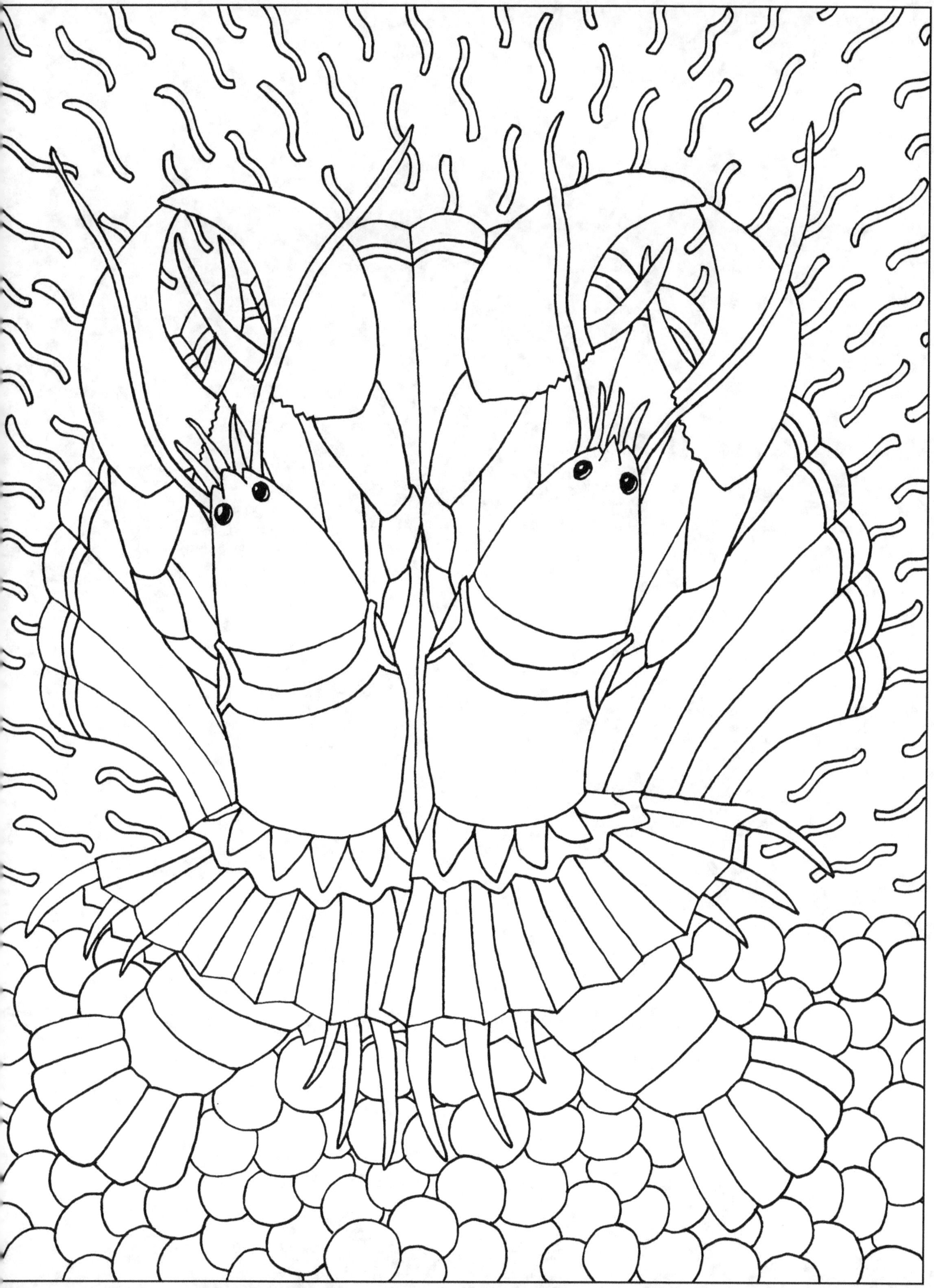

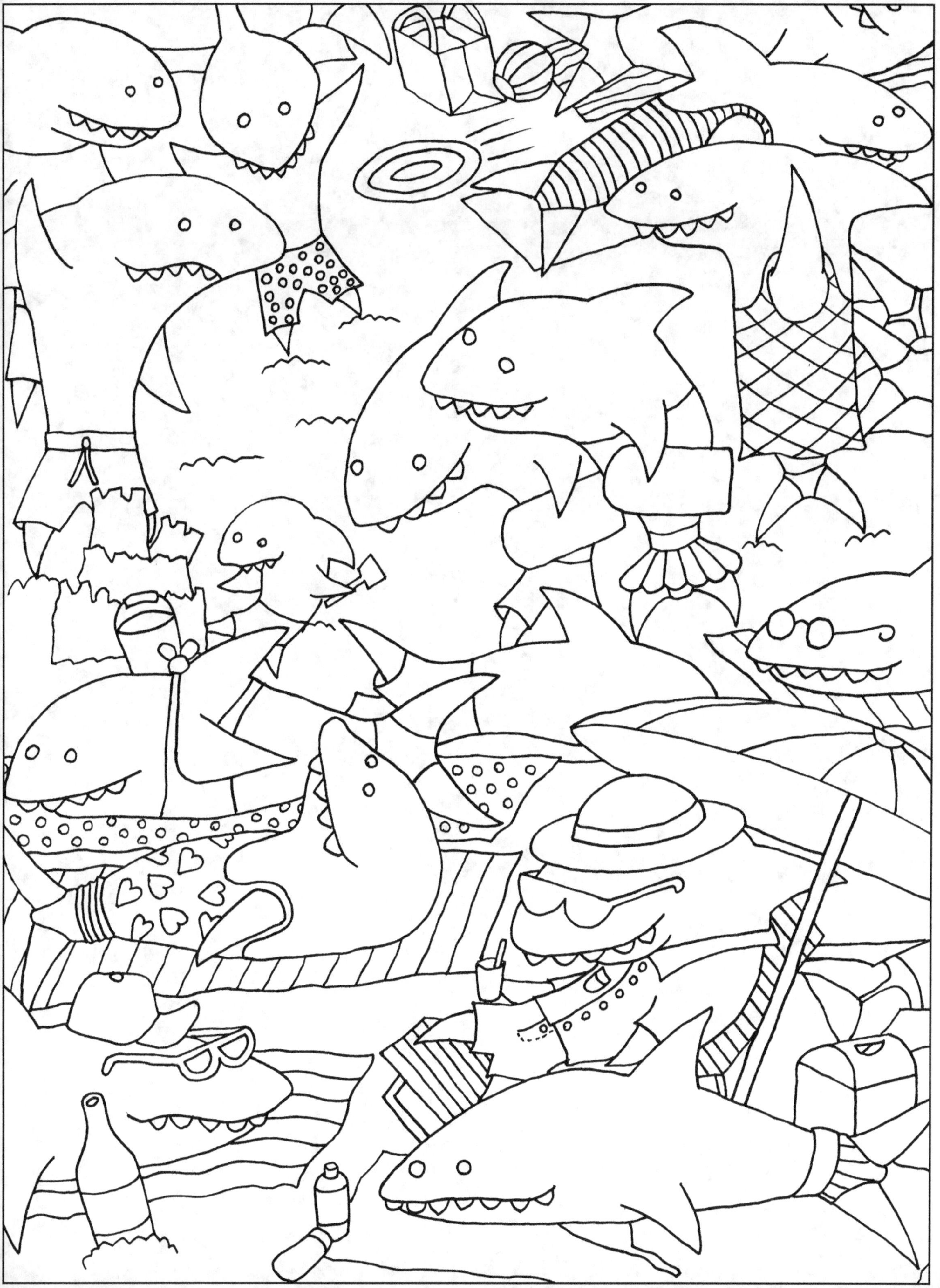

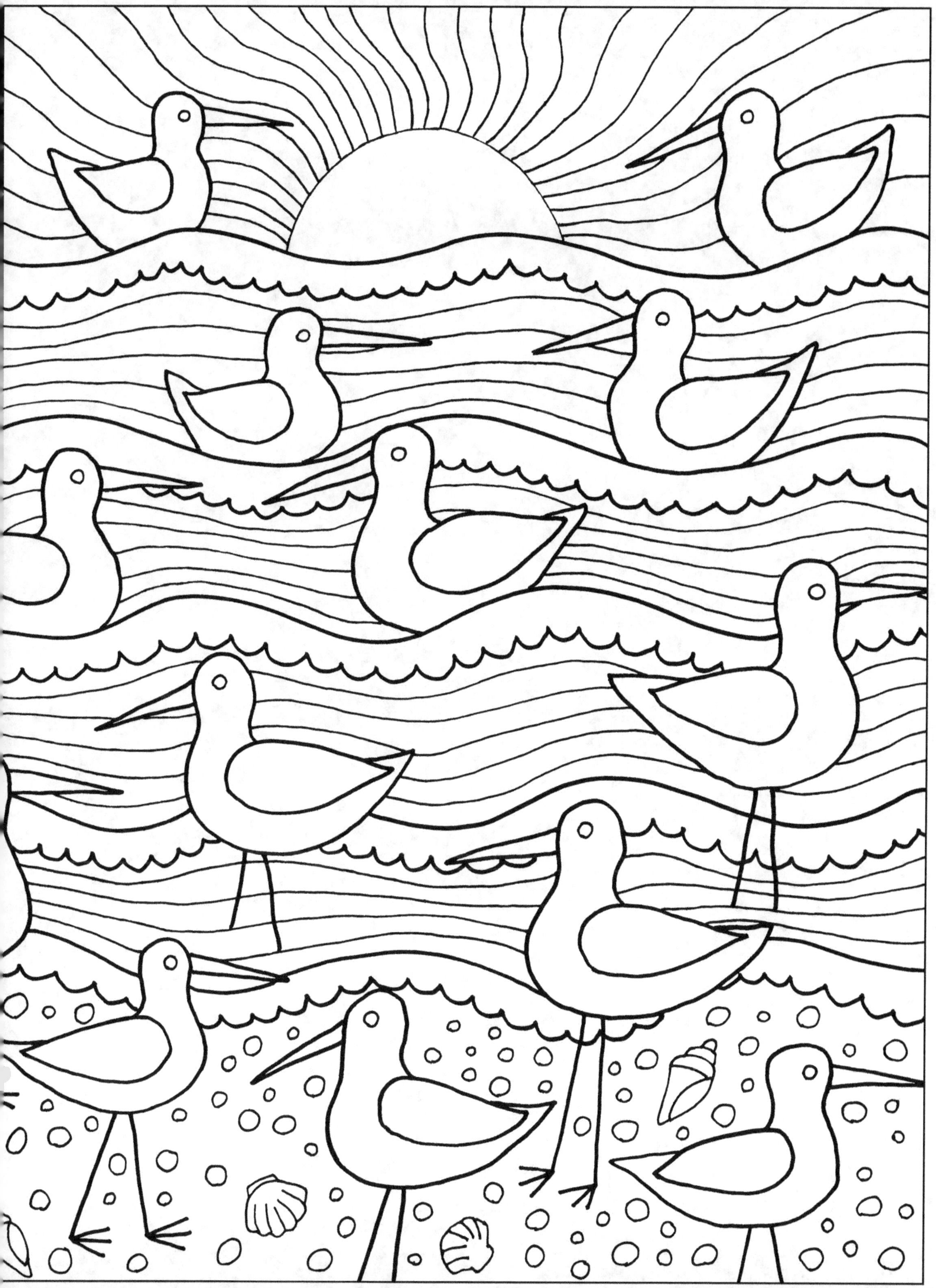

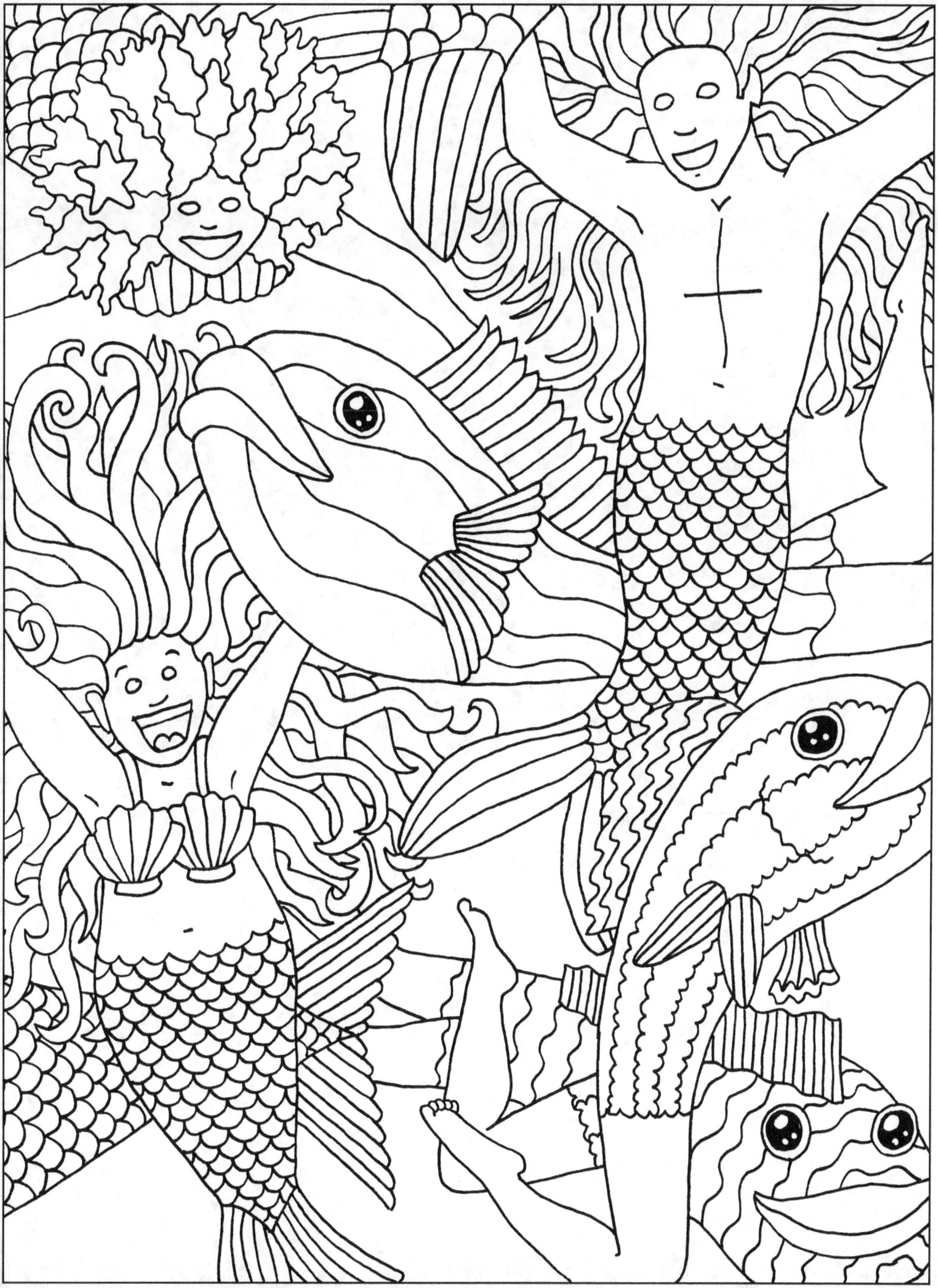

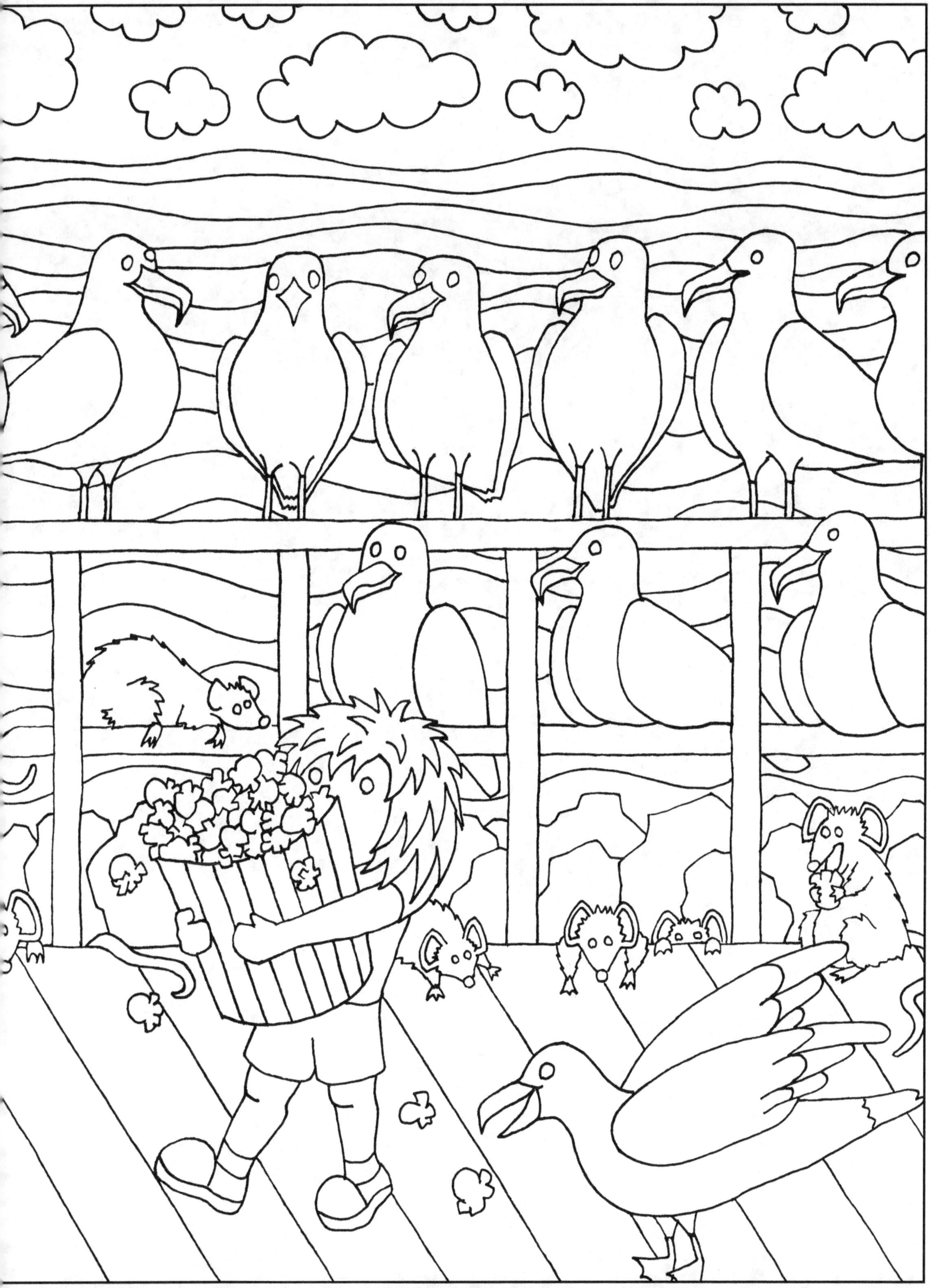

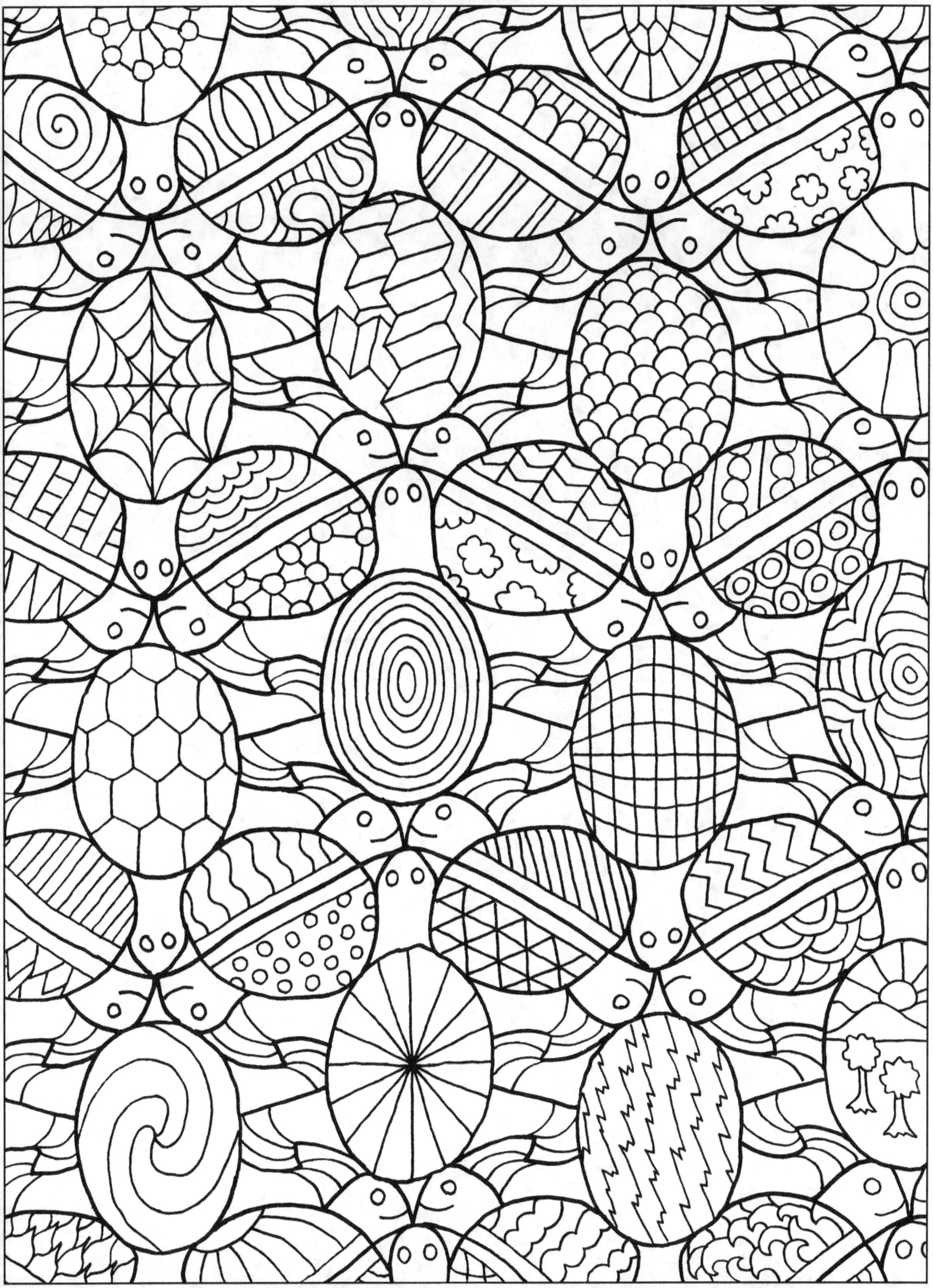

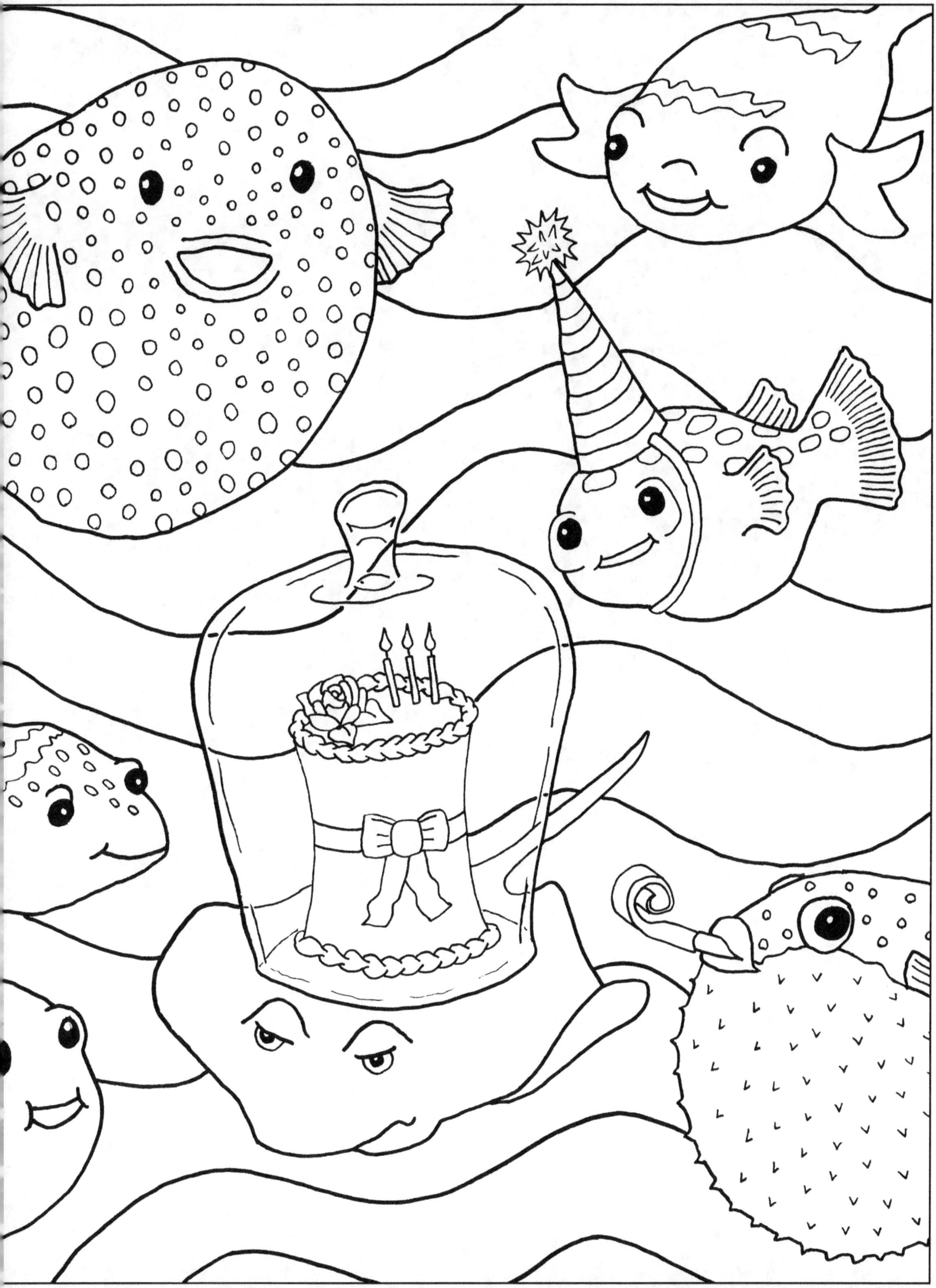

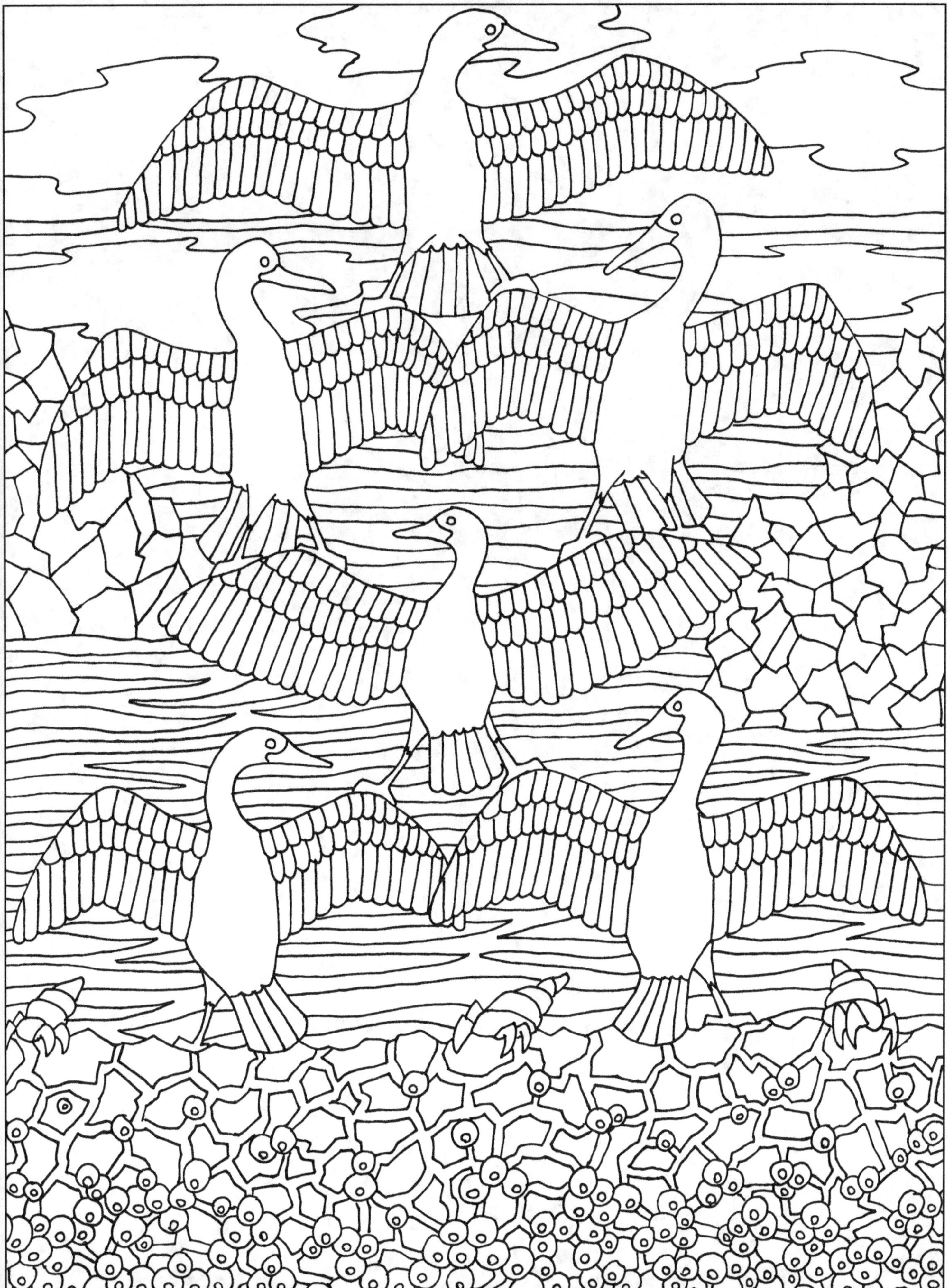

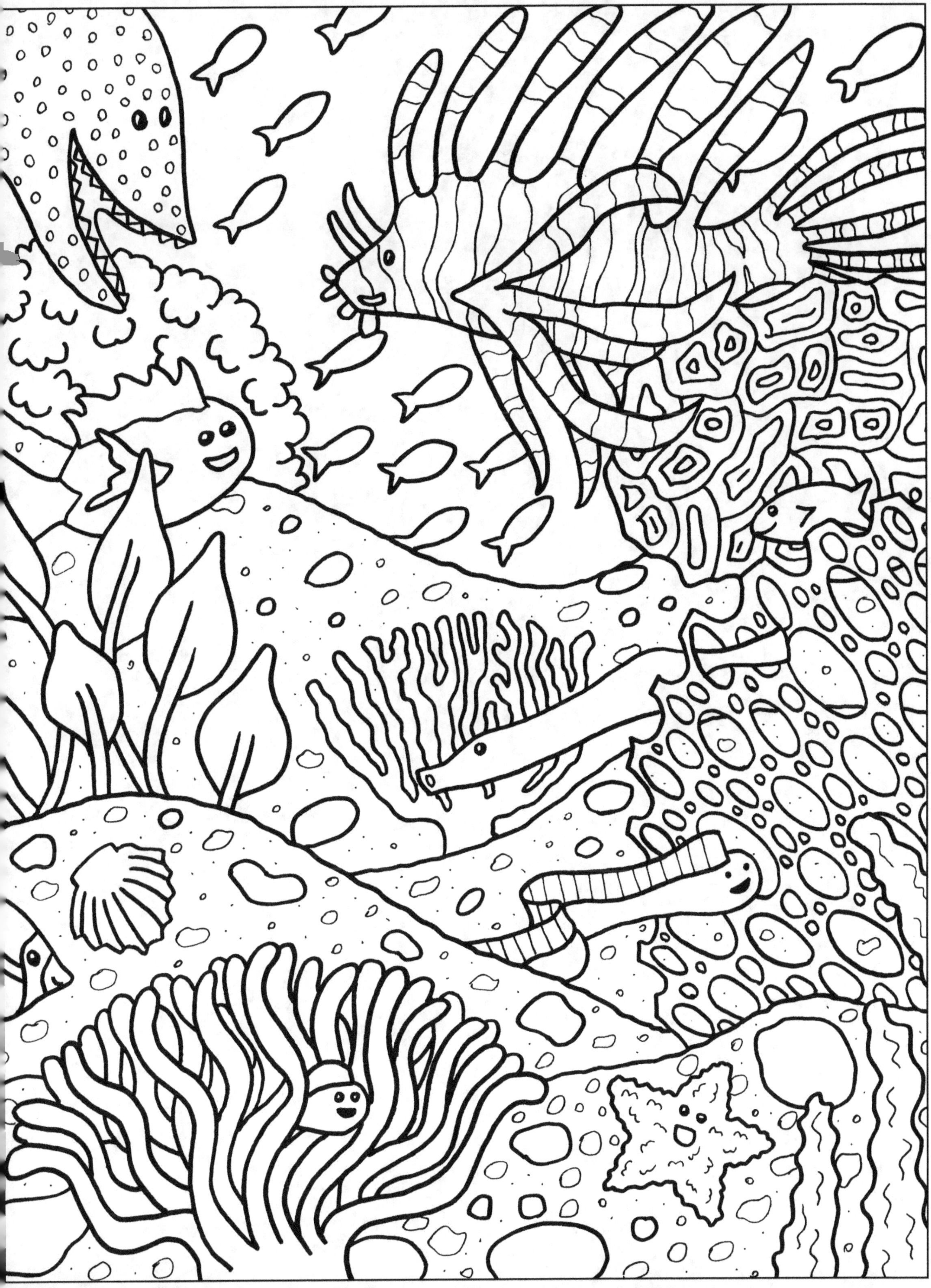

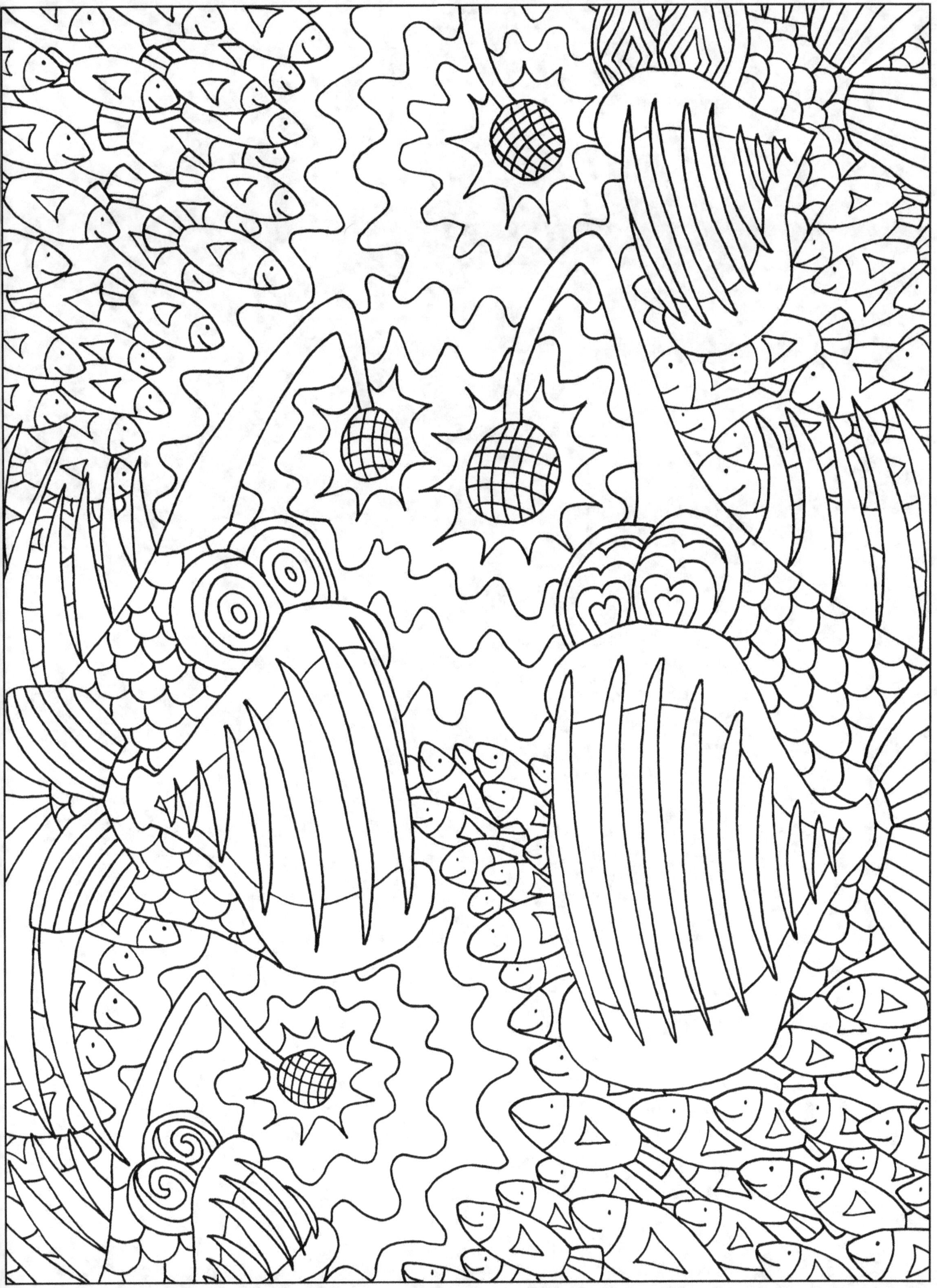

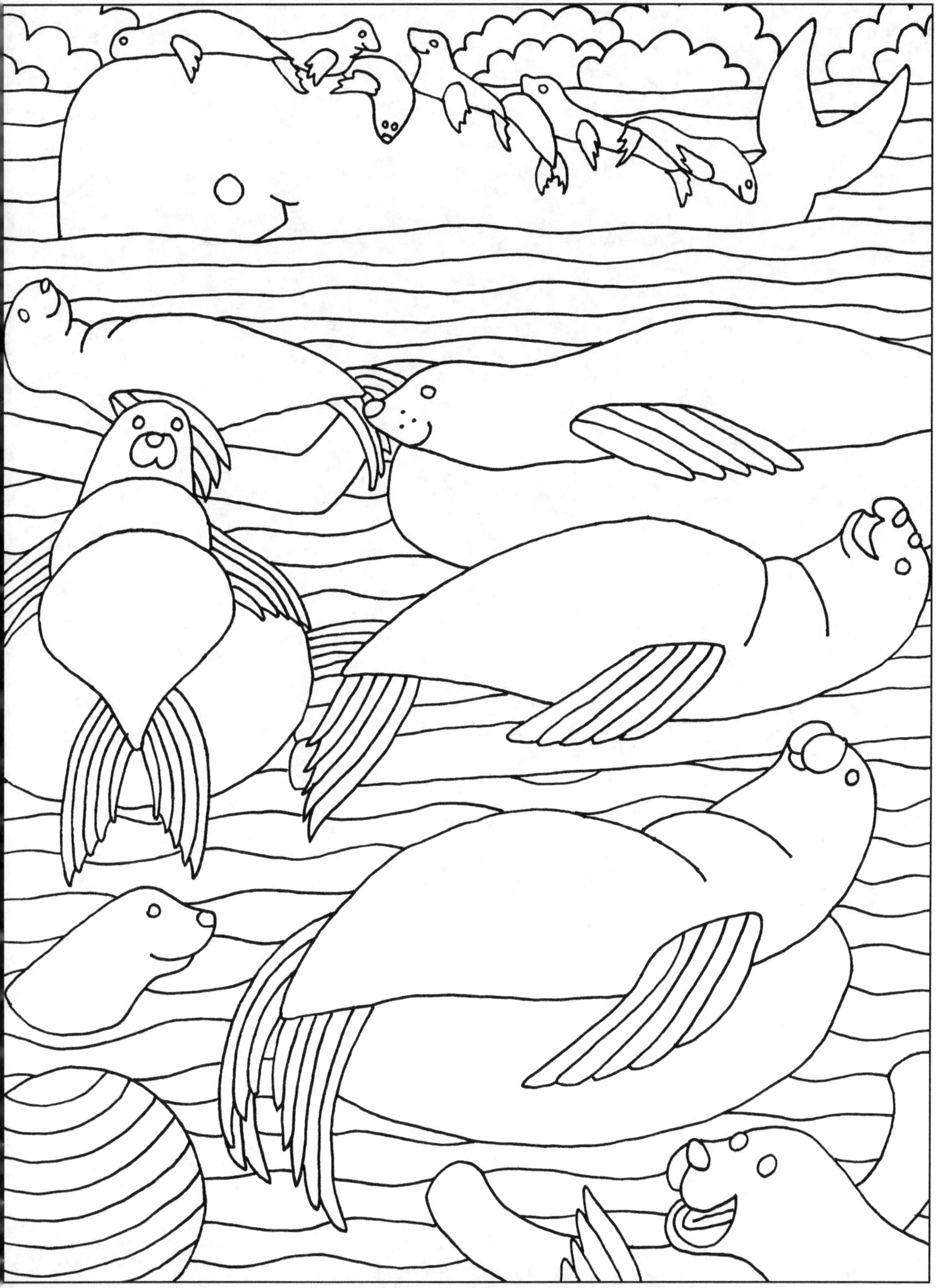

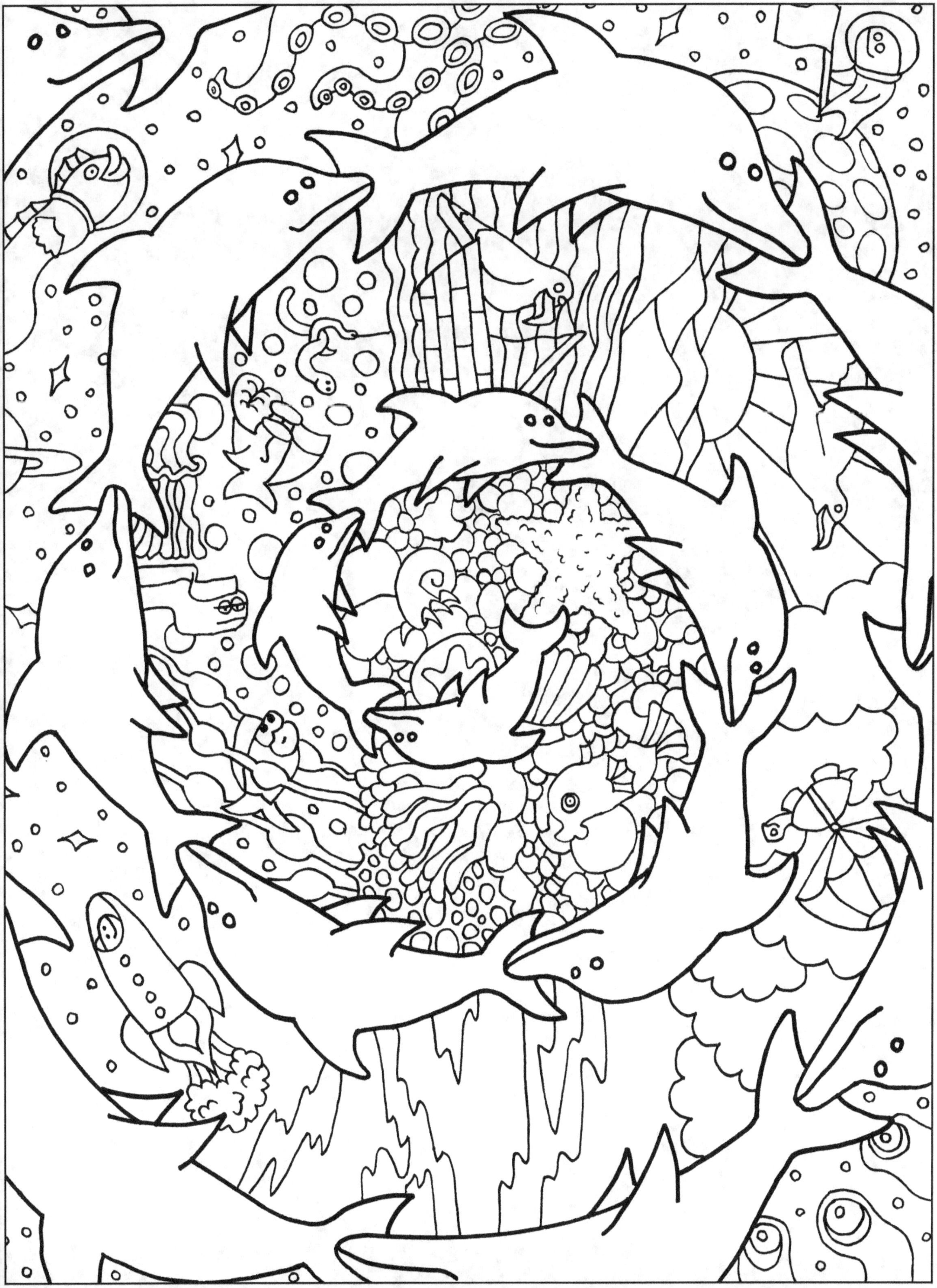

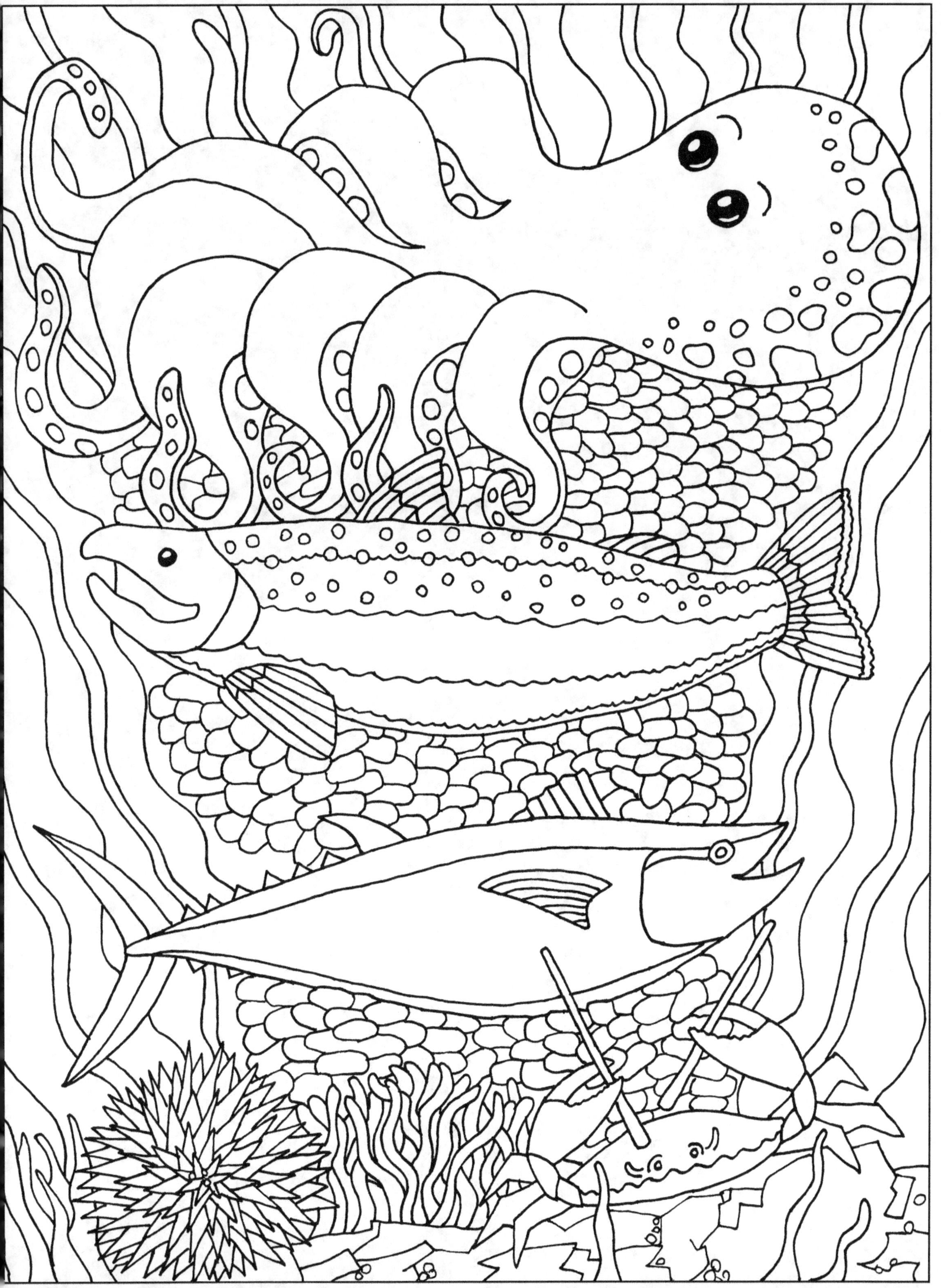

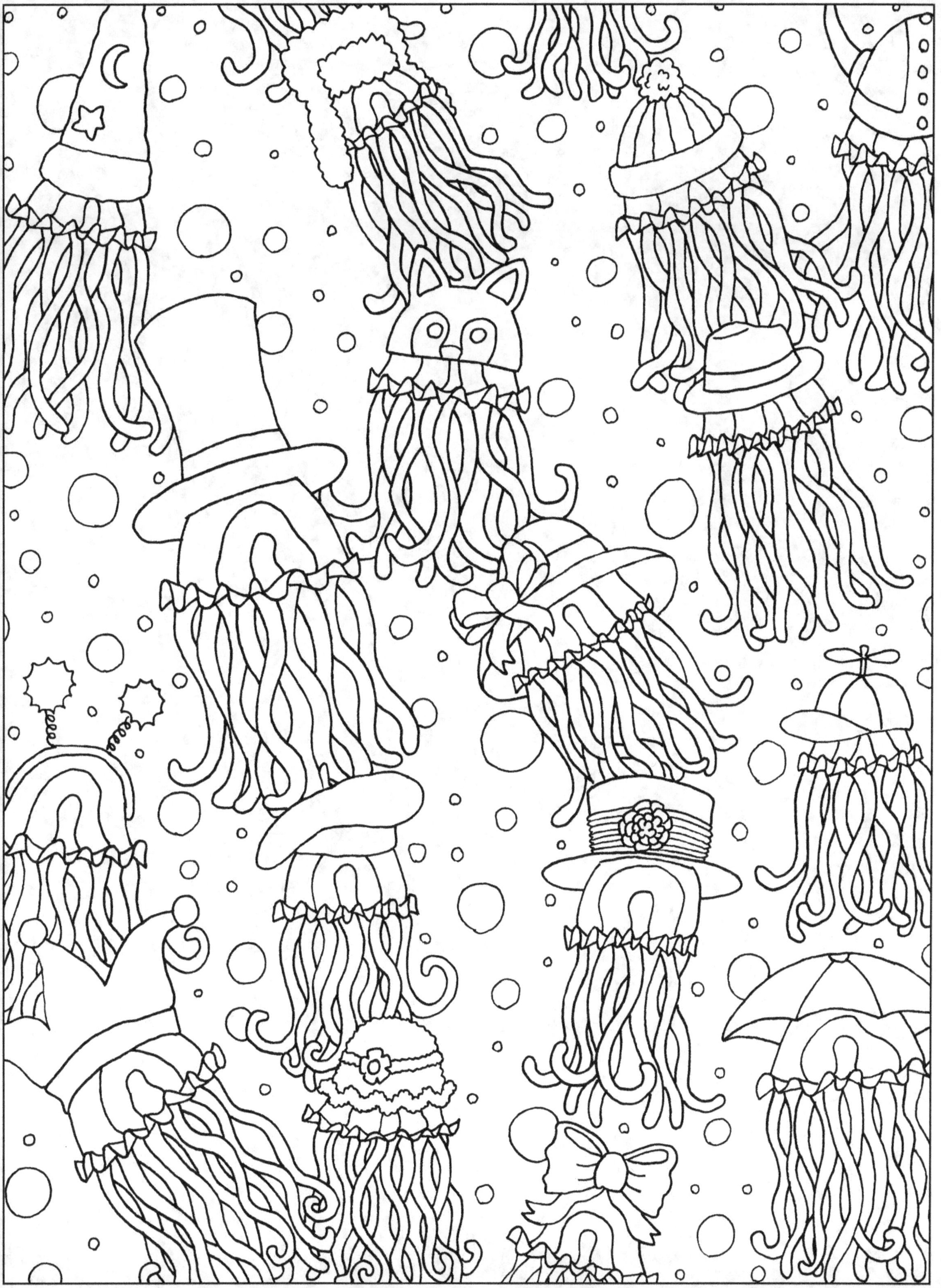

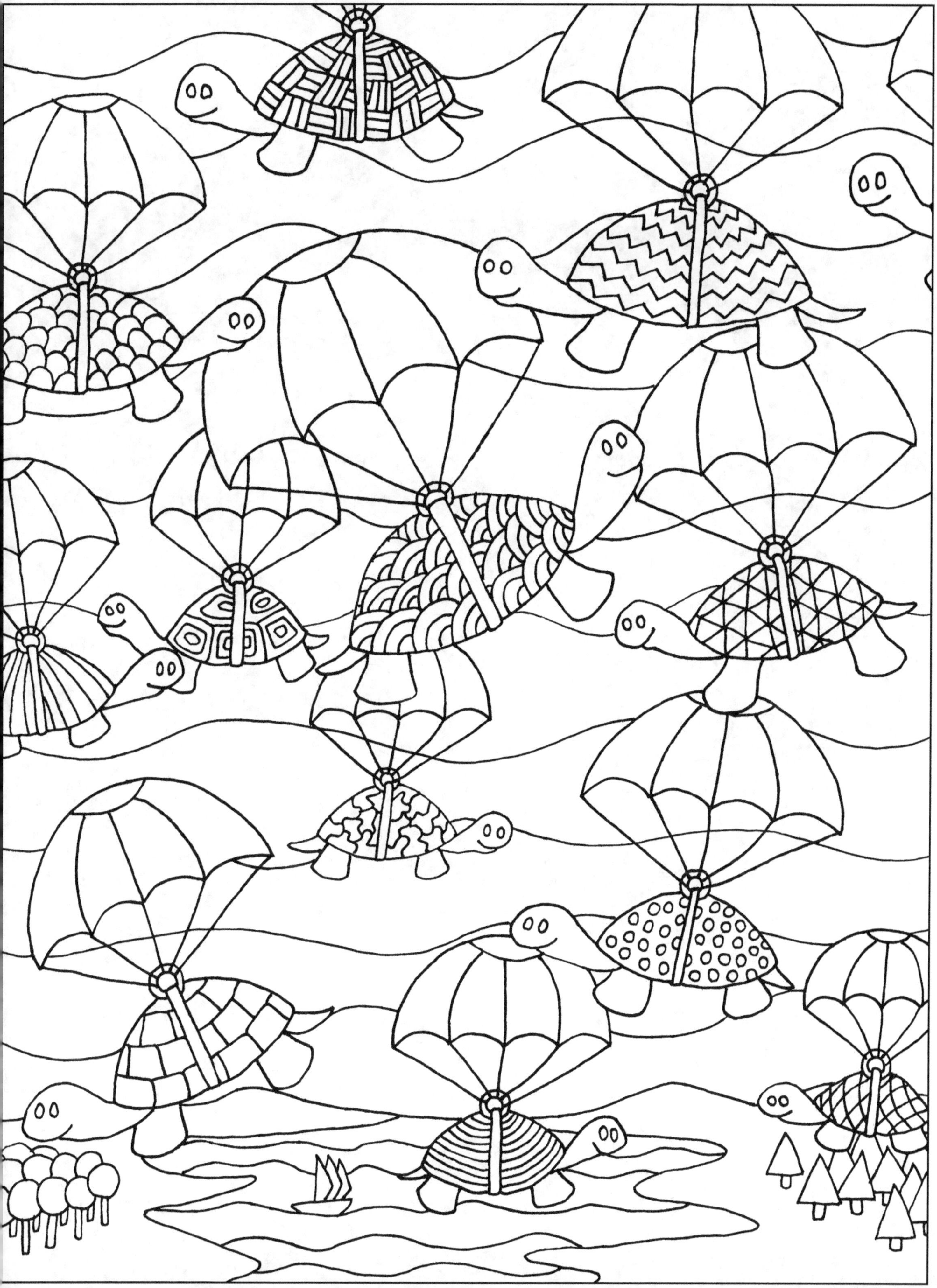

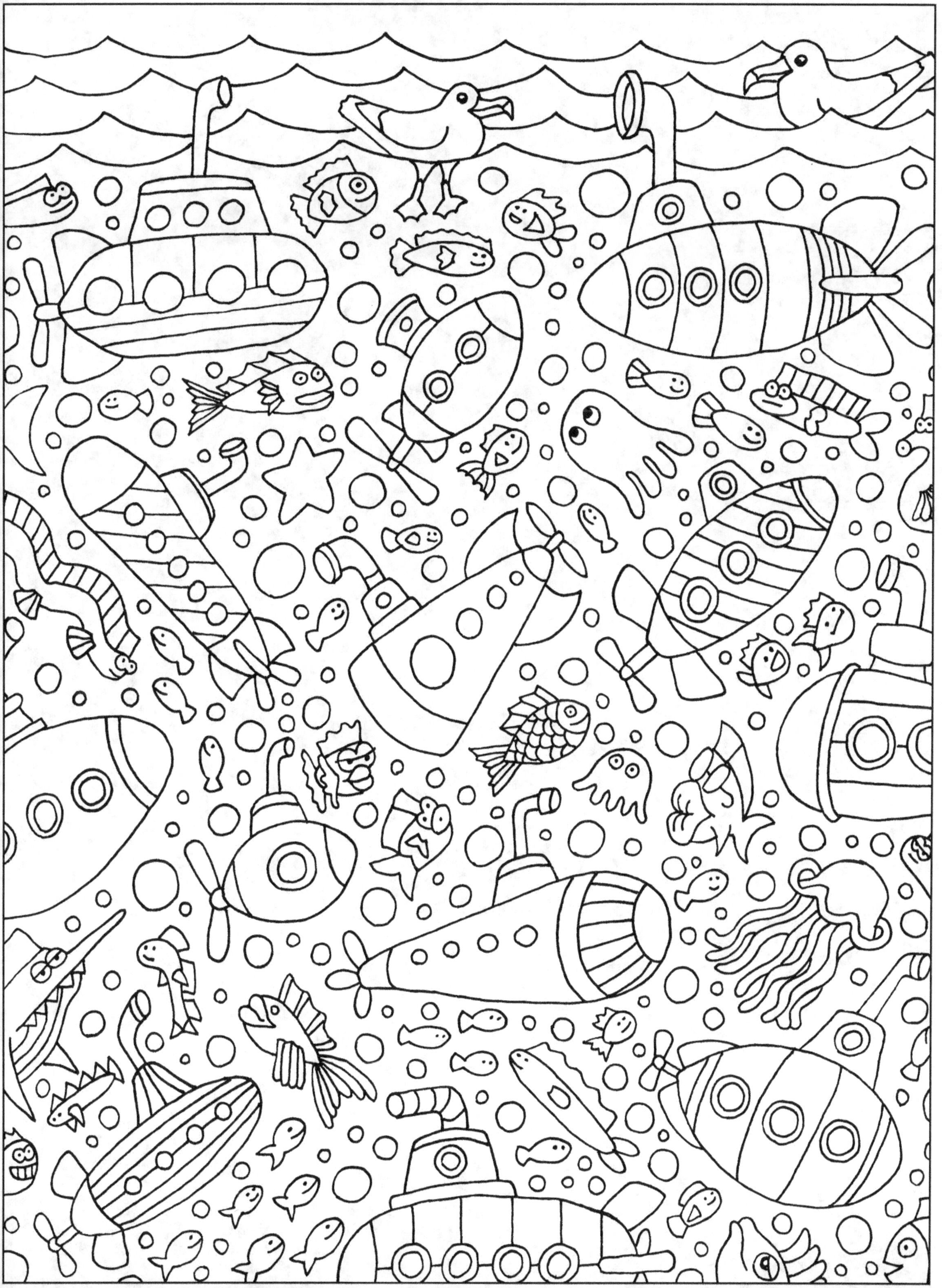

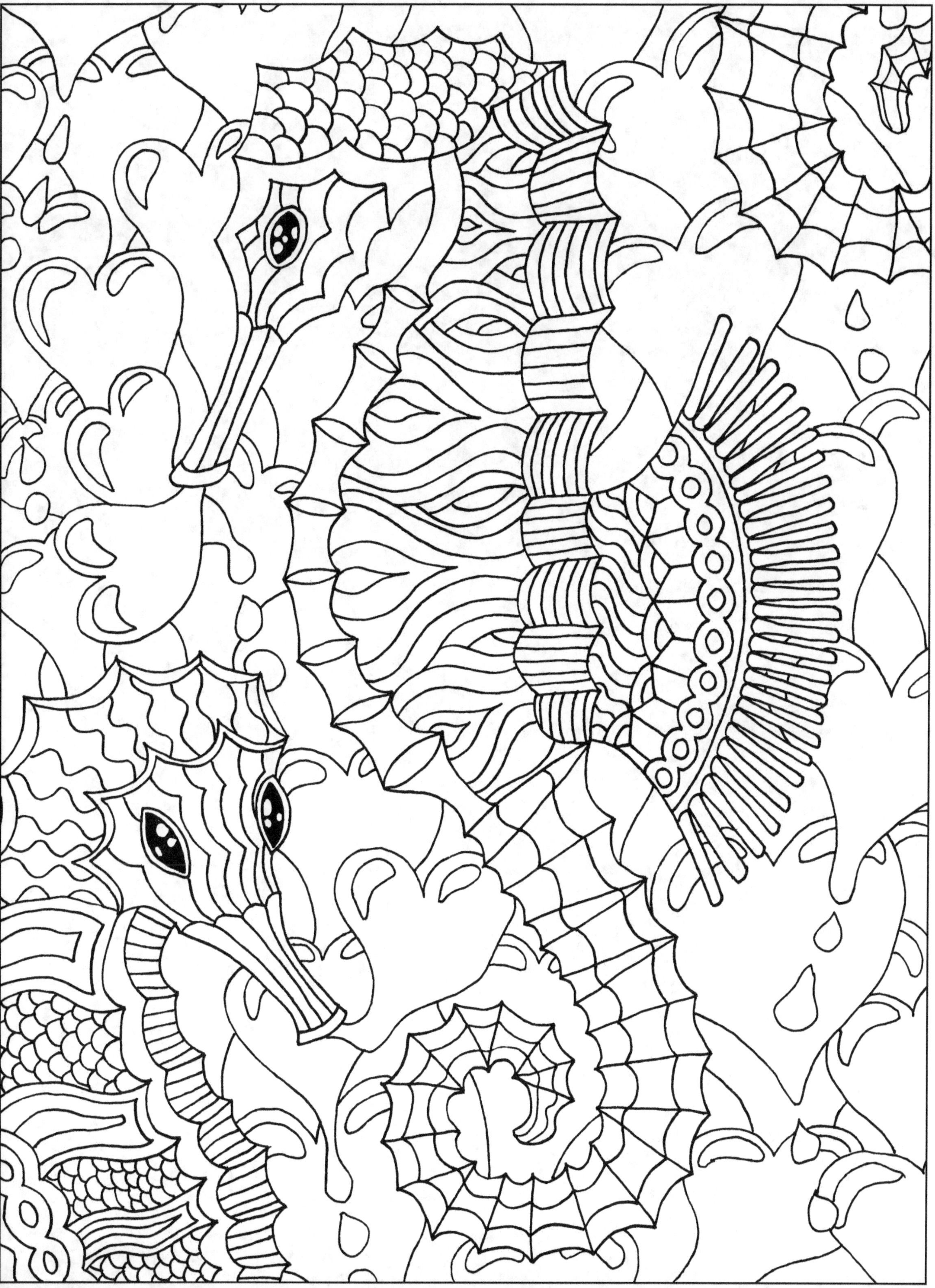

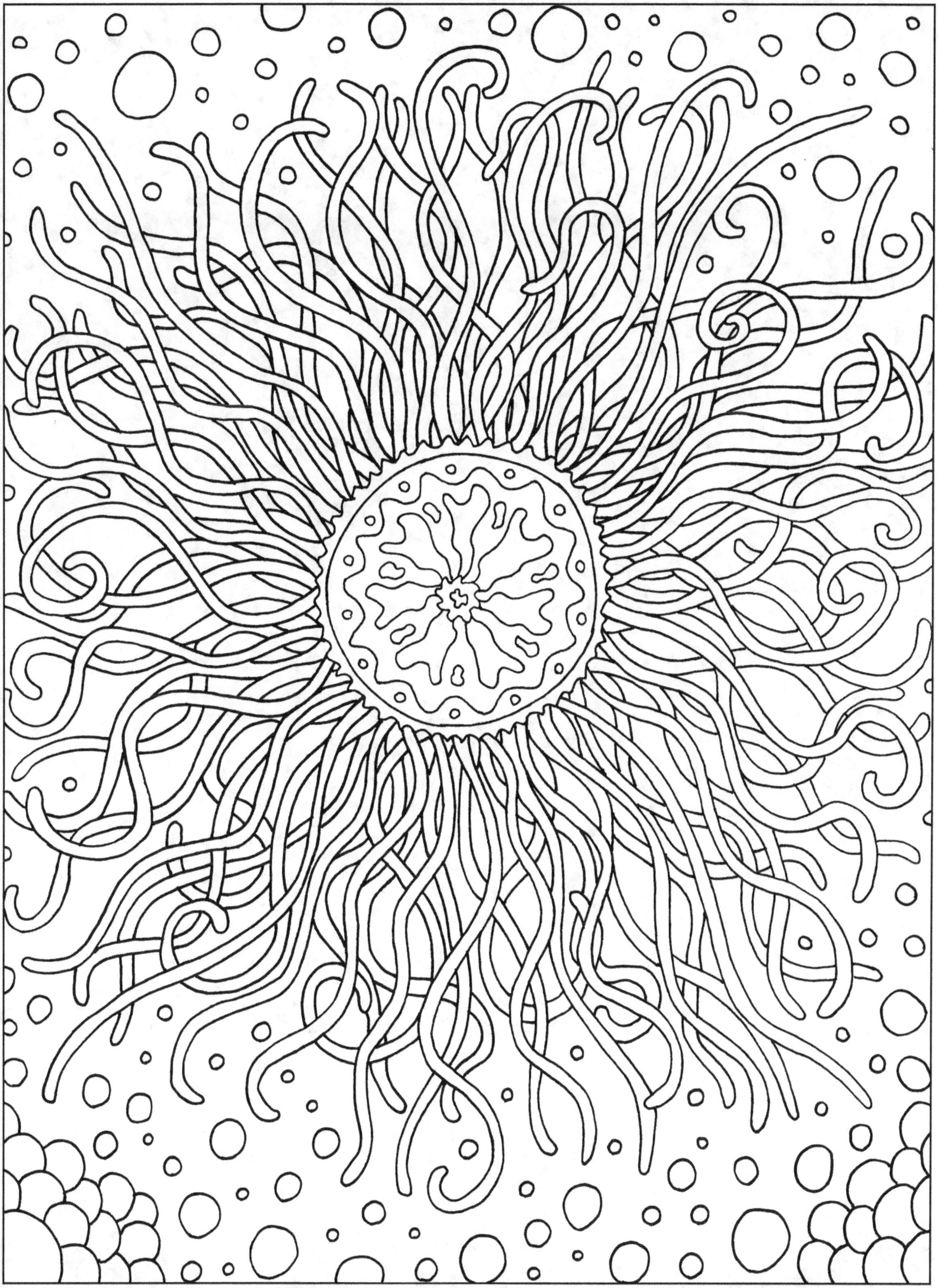

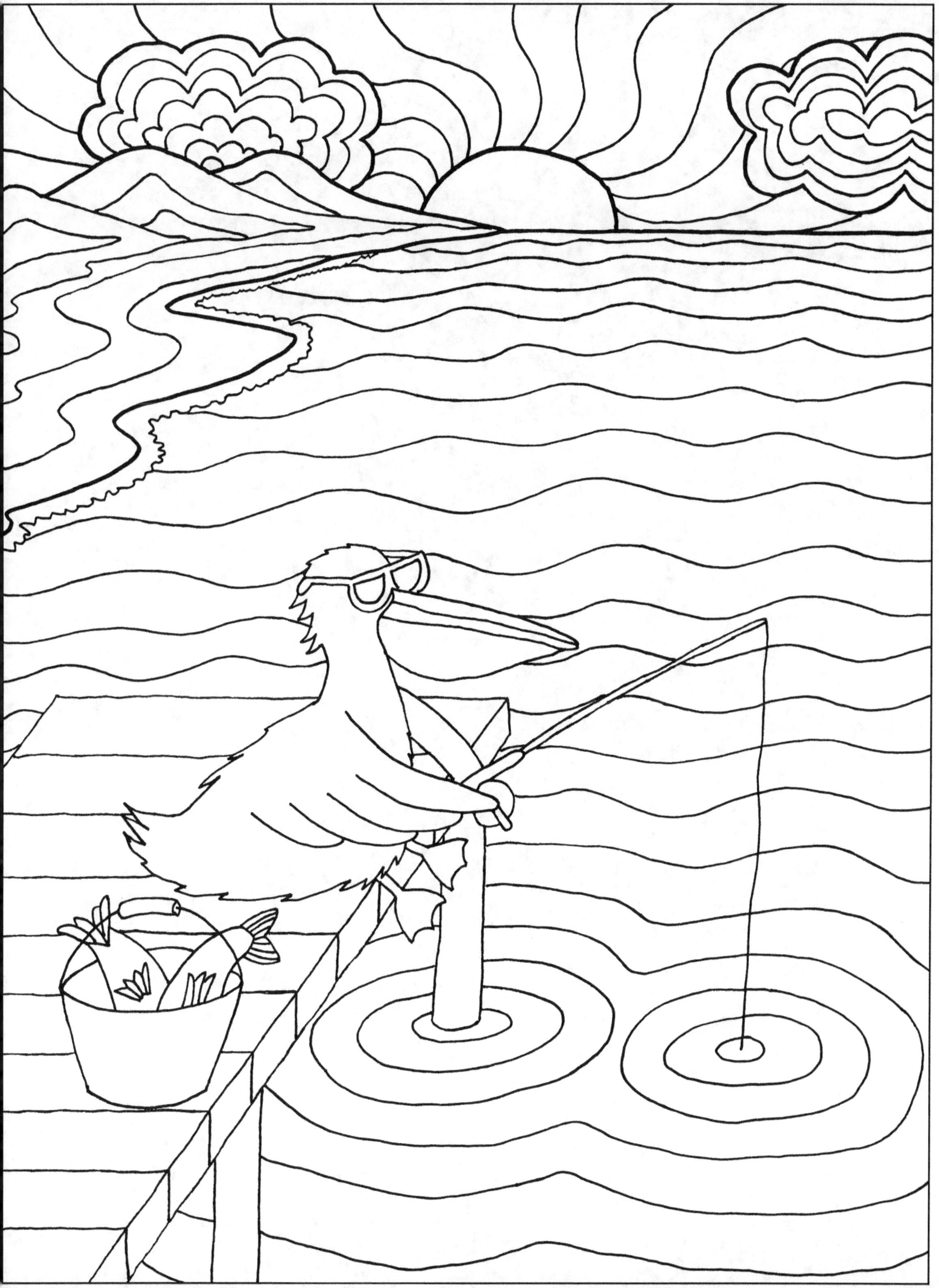

www.ingramcontent.com/pod-product-compliance
Lightning Source LLC
Chambersburg PA
CBHW081300180526
45170CB00007B/2504
* 9 7 8 1 5 3 9 9 7 4 6 0 4 *